# Dirty Jobs
# Exterminator

**Pamela McDowell**

www.av2books.com

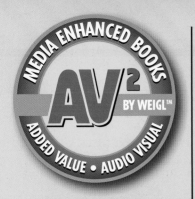

AV² provides enriched content that supplements and complements this book. Weigl's AV² books strive to create inspired learning and engage young minds in a total learning experience.

## Your AV² Media Enhanced books come alive with...

**Audio**
Listen to sections of the book read aloud.

**Key Words**
Study vocabulary, and complete a matching word activity.

Go to **www.av2books.com**, and enter this book's unique code.

**Video**
Watch informative video clips.

**Quizzes**
Test your knowledge.

## BOOK CODE

Q 9 0 1 8 3 3

**Embedded Weblinks**
Gain additional information for research.

**Slide Show**
View images and captions, and prepare a presentation.

**AV² by Weigl** brings you media enhanced books that support active learning.

**Try This!**
Complete activities and hands-on experiments.

**... and much, much more!**

Published by AV² by Weigl
350 5th Avenue, 59th Floor
New York, NY 10118
Websites: www.av2books.com      www.weigl.com

Library of Congress Control Number: 2014934855

ISBN 978-1-4896-0990-8 (hardcover)
ISBN 978-1-4896-0991-5 (softcover)
ISBN 978-1-4896-0992-2 (single-user eBook)
ISBN 978-1-4896-0993-9 (multi-user eBook)

Printed in the United States of America in North Mankato, Minnesota
1 2 3 4 5 6 7 8 9 0   18 17 16 15 14

042014
WEP150314

Project Coordinator: Aaron Carr
Designer: Mandy Christiansen

Every reasonable effort has been made to trace ownership and to obtain permission to reprint copyright material. The publishers would be pleased to have any errors or omissions brought to their attention so that they may be corrected in subsequent printings.

Weigl acknowledges Getty Images and iStockPhoto as primary image suppliers for this title.

# Contents

# What Is an Exterminator?

Exterminators are workers who get rid of pests in homes, schools, and places where people work. Scorpions, snakes, and other pests may be poisonous. Pests such as rats may make people sick. Some pests cause damage to buildings. Exterminators help keep people safe from these dangers.

Exterminators often specialize in controlling a few kinds of pests. Most deal with pests commonly found in homes, such as ants, roaches, and spiders. Some deal with problem animals, such as mice, bats, or raccoons.

## Many Names, One Job

Exterminators have many names. People also call them pest control workers. Some pest control workers specialize in a particular type of work. They may be fumigators, insecticide experts, termite technicians, or mosquito sprayers. Exterminators can run their own businesses. Others work with large pest control companies or even the government.

There were **68,400** pest control workers in the United States in 2010.

Termites cause more than **$5 billion** in damage every year in the United States.

More than **700** kinds of ants live in the United States.

Exterminators work to get rid of insects, molds, animals, and other harmful or unwanted pests. They use many different tools to do their jobs.

# Where They Work

**N**early 90 percent of exterminators work in businesses, homes, or other buildings. Exterminators may also work at schools, airports, ballparks, or high-rise buildings. They can work indoors or outdoors. Exterminators also work in all kinds of weather. Pest control workers travel to different places each day.

Exterminators carry heavy equipment and dangerous chemicals in their vehicles. They must store and manage these chemicals safely.

# 24 Hours a Day

In warm places, exterminators work year-round. Businesses and homeowners may have contracts with pest control companies. The contracts promise that exterminators will visit a home or business regularly to prevent problems with pests. It is common for pest control experts to work in the evening and on weekends. They may even get emergency calls. If a dangerous pest is found, an exterminator might be needed right away. An exterminator may be "on call." This means that he or she is ready to work 24 hours a day.

Exterminators often work in dark, dangerous places. They find trash, dirt, and possibly even chemicals.

Exterminators start each day in clean, fresh uniforms, but they often get dirty on the job.

# A Dirty Job

Fighting pests is a dirty job. Pests like to live in tight places where people rarely go. Often, pest controllers must climb into attics and crawl spaces to find the pests. Exterminators are able to identify pests by sight. They also look for droppings and nests. They search for the pests' food source. Exterminators try to remove the food source once they find it. It is hard to see dangers such as sharp objects. Even though they wear protective gear, these workers face risks from injury and disease.

## Pest Control Dangers

The most common pests in homes are controlled using **pesticides**. These chemicals are usually poisonous. Pest control experts must use them properly to stay safe. The workers must be careful not to breathe in the chemicals or their **fumes**. They must not let the chemicals touch their skin either. Exterminators work hard to keep themselves and other people safe.

Sometimes, a flashlight does not provide enough light for the exterminator to do his or her job. Professional pest control experts may need extra light to see into shadowy places.

Pests do not like to be bothered. They do not like people to take them away from their nests or food. Pests may sting or bite pest control experts while they work.

Pest control workers try to prevent damage. Experts look for the safest and most economical way to control pests.

Stinging insects inject poison into the skin. This causes burning, pain, itching, or other symptoms.

# Integrated Pest Management

Integrated Pest Management (IPM) is a strategy for looking at all parts of the pest control issue. Pest control workers first find out how the pests got into the building. They will estimate the damage that the pests have done. Then, they make an action plan to stop the pests from coming back.

A mouse can fit through a hole only 0.75 inches (1.9 centimeters) wide. That is the size of a **dime**.

**20** percent of Americans report they have seen bedbugs at home or in a hotel.

Pests need **food, shelter, and water** to live.

A female German roach can have **30,000** young in one year.

A colony of leaf-cutting ants can live in the same place for more than **60 years**.

# All in a Day's Work

**A**n exterminator's day usually begins in the office. Pest control workers find their appointments and routes for the day. When exterminators get to a work site, they inspect the building, take notes about what they find, and make a plan for removing the pests. Next, the pest control worker will either remove the pest or schedule a time to come back. Finally, the exterminator will give advice to keep the pest from coming back.

"Being an exterminator can be a good job," says Mark, a pest control worker from Phoenix, Arizona. "I work for a pest control company that works in homes and small businesses. Many people are afraid of the pests that I control. It makes me feel good knowing that I am helping to keep their homes healthy and safe. It can be a difficult job, though. I might be called in the middle of the night to get a skunk out of a basement or to remove a wasp nest on Sunday afternoon. Every day is different, and the job never gets boring."

In the United States, mosquitoes carry at least three diseases that can kill people.

The West Nile virus, which is spread by mosquitoes, first appeared in the United States in 1999.

A bedbug can live one year without eating.

Eliminating sources of moisture is an important part of pest control. Exterminators look for leaks or other water-related problems.

# Fumigating a Building

Sometimes, there are too many bugs to trap or spray. If so, the pest control workers need to treat the entire building. They put a tent over it. Then, workers pump pesticides into the building as fumes. The fumes kill the pests, and the gas goes away on its own. People cannot go back inside the building until the air is safe.

The fumigation process can take 24 to 72 hours, depending on the size of the building and the outdoor temperature.

# Staying Safe

Exterminators deal with many hazards in their work. They must work closely with pests that bite or sting. Some of the pests can be poisonous. Some carry diseases. Pest control workers risk exposure. The workers often handle dangerous chemicals. They have to wear proper safety equipment in order to stay safe on the job

### Protective coveralls

Pest control workers often wear disposable coverings. The special cloth in the coveralls protects the skin and clothing from dangerous chemicals. The disposable coveralls include a hood and shoe covers. The exterminator removes and disposes of the coveralls before moving to the next appointment. This keeps pests from spreading to a new place.

# Safety First

Federal and state governments have laws about the use of pesticides. Pest control workers complete special training to use pesticides. They must use proper safety gear at all times. Pesticide companies help the workers learn how to use their products correctly.

## Respirator

Things in the air can be dangerous for pest control workers. A respirator can filter 99 percent of dust, bacteria, and chemicals from the air. The respirator is worn during inspection and when using pesticides.

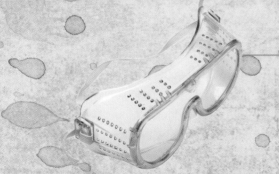

## Goggles

The chemicals in pesticides can make the eyes red, itchy, and watery. They can even cause permanent damage. Goggles help prevent this. They also protect the eyes from dust in places such as attics and crawl spaces.

## Chemical-resistant gloves

Gloves protect the exterminator from bites and stings. They are made of a fabric that also protects skin. Without gloves, the harsh chemicals could cause burns.

# Tools of the Trade

**P**est control experts use a variety of equipment in their work. All pest control workers use a flashlight to start a job. A flashlight is useful in finding and identifying the pest. The light makes scratches and chew marks easy to see. An **ultraviolet flashlight** shows even more signs of pests. Scorpions glow in ultraviolet light. Urine from rodents, such as mice and rats, glows blue or yellow in ultraviolet light.

## Exterminator Tools

Once pest control workers find out what kind of pest is in the building, they must choose the right equipment. Sometimes, they will have the things they need on their truck. Other times, they will need to come back for a second appointment.

### Flashlight

A flashlight allows pest control workers to see into dark spaces when they look for pests. Flashlights help workers look for signs of pests, like their homes or their droppings.

### Sprayer

Workers use sprayers if the pests are in small places. They spray pesticides with the sprayer. These chemicals are dangerous. Workers must use them carefully.

## Traps

Traps work well in places with fewer pests. The traps may be sticky, spring-operated, or electronic. Sometimes, pest control workers use multi-catch traps. These can remove many snakes or rodents at once. They use catch-and-release traps for larger pests such as squirrels and raccoons. The pest control workers release the animals later in a more suitable place.

## Vacuum

Pest control workers use a special vacuum to clean up insects. It also cleans up the mess that the insects make. A vacuum can get rid of cockroaches and bedbugs.

In the 19th century, people used natural products to get rid of insect pests. They used kerosene and nicotine for pest control. Scientists discovered strong chemicals, such as **DDT**, during World War II. These chemicals worked well, but they were unhealthy for people and animals. They were especially harmful to fish and birds.

# Now

More people want to use natural products that do less harm to the environment. Products such as **diatomaceous earth** work well to control insects. At low strengths, diatomaceous earth does not harm mammals. No-kill traps, devices that do not harm animals, are a **humane** option for mammal pests.

# The Role of the Exterminator

**P**est control is an important part of keeping a community healthy and safe. Workers must remove pests quickly. Their actions protect people and buildings. This also stops the spread of diseases caused by pests, such as rabies. Without pest control, **food processors** and restaurants could not provide clean, healthy food. Hospitals would spread diseases instead of cure them. The exterminator's role is to help prevent these problems. People count on pest control workers to make the area safe again.

# Preventing Pest Problems

An exterminator does more than just rid areas of bugs or rodents. People who are thinking about buying a property may have a pest control worker inspect it first. The pest control expert will describe signs of pest problems in a report. He or she may also suggest ways to prevent problems. This includes using screens on windows, vents, and fireplaces. The exterminator may also suggest clearing plants and other items at least 18 inches (46 cm) away from the **foundation** of the building.

> Sometimes, pest control experts treat the outside of the building. This can keep many unwelcome pests out of the home.

## Big Pests, Big Problems

Bugs and rodents are not the only pests that exterminators must control. Bats, raccoons, and skunks sometimes make their homes in buildings. They may carry a sickness called **rabies**. Flying squirrels, opossums, and snakes can also become problems. However, some of these animals are endangered, so an exterminator must know about laws that protect the animals.

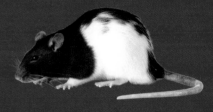

A raccoon can squeeze through a hole **4.5** inches (11.25 cm) wide.

*Each year, nearly 40,000 people in the United States come in contact with an animal that has rabies.*

Federal laws protect the **21 kinds** of woodpeckers in the United States. They can cause damage to homes by pecking holes in siding, but it is illegal to destroy them.

**There are about 40 species of bats in the United States.**

# Becoming an Exterminator

To become an exterminator, one needs to have the right training. A high school diploma is required in most places. A person may need to complete an approved course and exam. Pest control workers learn other skills on the job during an **apprenticeship**. Many areas require pest control workers to have a special **license**. They must also prove they have never been convicted of crimes to become bonded. Being bonded means that the company will cover the cost of any damage done by workers as they do their job.

**Salaries** for pest control workers vary across the United States. There is a greater need for pest control in warmer areas and in larger cities. Workers often earn more in these places. The chart below shows the average yearly salary for different jobs within the pest control industry.

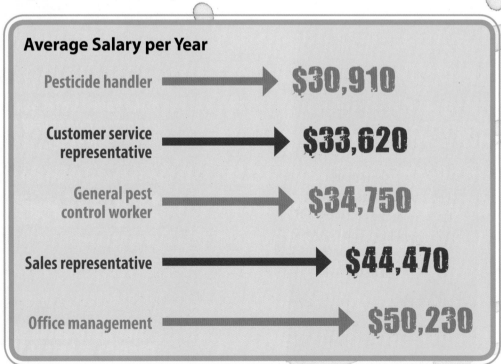

**Average Salary per Year**

| | |
|---|---|
| Pesticide handler | $30,910 |
| Customer service representative | $33,620 |
| General pest control worker | $34,750 |
| Sales representative | $44,470 |
| Office management | $50,230 |

The United States government predicts that the number of pest control jobs will increase by 20 percent by 2022.

# Is This Career for You?

**A** career as an exterminator is demanding. It involves working in tight spaces with strong chemicals. Much of the work is dirty and dangerous. An exterminator fills an important role in the daily life of a community. Protecting the health and safety of other people can be a rewarding job. Experts believe there will probably be about 26 percent more jobs in the pest control industry by 2020.

## ✓ Training

Pest control workers continue to train throughout their careers. This training includes the use of new equipment and chemicals. An exterminator may also train in a specialized area of pest control, such as fumigation or mosquito control.

## ✓ Education

A high school diploma and completion of an approved course are usually required. Almost half of all pest control workers in the United States have gone to college or earned a degree.

## ✓ Application

Contact pest control companies directly to apply. Some exterminators look after government buildings. To apply for this kind of position, contact the federal or state government. Many companies advertise job openings on the internet.

# Career Connections

Plan your exterminator career with this activity. Follow the instructions outlined in the steps to complete the process of becoming an exterminator.

 **1.** Speak to a pest control worker in your community. This person can describe local pests. He or she can answer your questions, as well.

 **2.** Visit a job fair or a university career center to learn about working in the pest control industry.

 **3.** Work on your resumé. A good resumé that shows your strongest skills can go a long way toward attracting the attention of potential employers.

 **4.** Call or write to a pest control company. Say that you are interested in an exterminator position. Ask for advice on how to apply.

1. Decide if you have the personality and attitude for eliminating pests. If you do not mind a dirty job, are in good physical shape, and can carefully follow instructions, this may be the job for you.

2. Consider the qualifications you must have, such as a driver's license. A good understanding of science and math will be a bonus.

3. Contact employers for requirements. Look for private and public pest control companies. Get in touch with them and find out what they are looking for from job seekers.

4. Apply for the position and arrange an interview. If the employer contacts you, come to the interview with knowledge of the industry and your skills.

# Quiz

**1.** What insect causes billions of dollars worth of damages every year in the United States?

**2.** What are the chemicals that exterminators use called?

**3.** What mammal can fit through a hole the size of a dime?

**4.** What safety equipment do exterminators use?

**5.** What is the exterminator's most important piece of equipment?

**6.** How many people are exposed to rabies each year in the United States?

**7.** What portion of pest control workers in the United States have attended college or have earned a degree?

**8.** Why is it important for an exterminator to be able to follow instructions carefully?

**9.** What are the most common pests an exterminator deals with?

**10.** How does an exterminator eliminate pests from an entire building?

**Answers: 1.** Termites
**2.** Pesticides **3.** A mouse
**4.** Respirator, goggles, coveralls, gloves **5.** Flashlight **6.** 40,000
**7.** 50 percent **8.** To prepare and use chemicals properly
**9.** Ants, cockroaches, spiders
**10.** Fumigates it

# Key Words

**apprenticeship:** time spent learning a skill from an expert

**DDT:** dichlorodiphenyltrichloroethane; helped control malaria and protected crops until scientists realized that it was harmful to the environment

**diatomaceous earth:** a powder made of sharp, microscopic bits of algae fossils

**food processors:** companies and businesses that prepare and package food for stores and restaurants

**foundation:** the solid base on which a home or other building is built

**fumes:** harmful gas or smoke

**humane:** not cruel to people or animals

**license:** permission from the government to work in some business or profession pesticides: chemicals that kill pests, especially insects

**pesticides:** chemicals used to kill pests

**rabies:** a deadly disease that can be carried by wild animals such as squirrels, raccoons, or bats.

**salaries:** the amount of money people are paid each year for doing their jobs

**ultraviolet flashlight:** a type of light that cannot be seen by the human eye

# Index

# Log on to www.av2books.com

AV² by Weigl brings you media enhanced books that support active learning. Go to www.av2books.com, and enter the special code found on page 2 of this book. You will gain access to enriched and enhanced content that supplements and complements this book. Content includes video, audio, weblinks, quizzes, a slide show, and activities.

## AV² Online Navigation

**Book Pages**
AV² pages directly correspond to pages in the book.

**Audio**
Listen to sections of the book read aloud.

**Video**
Watch informative video clips.

**Key Words**
Study vocabulary, and complete a matching word activity.

**Embedded Weblinks**
Gain additional information for research.

**Quizzes**
Test your knowledge.

**Slide Show**
View images and captions, and prepare a presentation.

**Try This!**
Complete activities and hands-on experiments.

AV² was built to bridge the gap between print and digital. We encourage you to tell us what you like and what you want to see in the future.

## Sign up to be an AV² Ambassador at www.av2books.com/ambassador.

Due to the dynamic nature of the Internet, some of the URLs and activities provided as part of AV² by Weigl may have changed or ceased to exist. AV² by Weigl accepts no responsibility for any such changes. All media enhanced books are regularly monitored to update addresses and sites in a timely manner. Contact AV² by Weigl at 1-866-649-3445 or av2books@weigl.com with any questions, comments, or feedback.